The Light Above, the Colors Within

A Mandala Coloring Book with Chakra-Inspired Poems and Affirmations

Written by

Carol J. Mahsem

BALBOA.
PRESS

A DIVISION OF HAY HOUSE

Balboa Press books may be ordered through booksellers or by contacting:

Balboa Press
A Division of Hay House
1663 Liberty Drive
Bloomington, IN 47403
www.balboapress.com
1 (877) 407-4847

ISBN: 978-1-5043-7242-8 (sc)
ISBN: 978-1-5043-7241-1 (e)

Print information available on the last page.

Balboa Press rev. date: 01/17/2017

Note From the Author,

The poems and affirmations contained in this coloring book are an inspiration I had after satisfying my desire to learn something about the Chakras. They are my interpretation based on information I gathered from various readings. I am not an expert on the subject, rather I'm perhaps someone not unlike yourself; someone looking for answers about my own spiritual journey.

My hope is that the poems and affirmations will inspire you to seek guidance from 'The Light Above' and encourage you to explore 'The Colors Within' and perhaps investigate for yourself the many books available on the Chakras.

I offer up this small collection with the sincere wish that you will enjoy the readings and the mandalas.

Peace and Love,

Carol

Thank you

First and foremost, I need to thank the Universe for the inspiration and guidance I received throughout this endeavor.

I also want to Thank...

My husband Andy for his love and unwavering faith and encouragement.

My daughters Maggie and Katie for believing in me, and for offering their honest feedback and suggestions.

My dear friends Vicki and Kelly for being supportive of my idea and for encouraging me to 'do more'.

Dedication

*This coloring book is dedicated to
My granddaughters Rosemary and Sophia
the 'Loves of my Life'.*

Contents

The Chakras,
The Poems,
and
The Affirmations

Root (Muladhara) Chakra

Symbol: Four petal Lotus flower

Location: Base of spine

Primary Drive: Survival

Color: Red

Element: Earth

Sense: Smell

Associated Crystals: Ruby, Garnet, Obsidian

The First Chakra

I wait.

Then, pushed into existence, I cry out, red faced and set,
I instinctively know how to get my needs met.

The force that drives me, ruby red at the base,
I come into this world, this Human race.

I'm part of the earth, but now I'm out,
My roots still connected, but I know how to shout
Feed me! Warm me! Love me! Keep me dry!
I'm all survival; I will not die.

I have no alliance; allegiance to none.
My only purpose to reach for the sun,
upward, ever reaching, stretching, and striving!
Always about me; this force that is driving.

Faith or Fear? That's the test I will face;
move onward and upward?
Or stay at the base.

Trust or defend? Go forward or retreat;
My face turned skyward, Mother Earth at my feet.

I have to stay balanced; a delicate dance,
But I must move upward, I must advance.

Here at the root, the Divine up above,
I have so much to learn about Faith, Trust, and Love.

I go forward, fall back, try again, always trying.
I rise and I fall, sometimes feeling like dying
and remaining forever in the darkness below...

But The Light is above;
The Divine I must know.

The First Chakra Affirmation

I'm struggling now
and it's hard to think of enjoying life
when I'm not sure if
I can get through another day.

Please give me clarity
so that I may know
what I need to do
for myself, my family,
or any other individual who's
well being is dependent
upon my ability to provide.

Give me the strength to
get past my fears of failing
and give me the confidence
I need to succeed.

Help me find a way to
re-connect with Mother Earth
so my fears can be
calmed by Her nurturing heart,
and faith in myself
can be restored.

Sacral (Svadisthana) Chakra

Symbol: Six petal Lotus flower

Location: Center of abdomen

Primary drive: Pleasure

Color: Orange

Element: Water

Sense: Taste

Associated Crystals: Carnilian, Amber

The Second Chakra

I begin.

Warmth, satisfaction, feeling so right;
I bask in the glow of carnelian light.

This life that is mine with all of it's pleasures;
wherever I turn, the worlds full of treasures
and things to enjoy; the good and the bad,
my only goal is to never feel sad.

The sights, the smells, the taste, the sensation;
all here for me without reservation.

But wait.
Here too I must balance and try to stay steady;
if I fall off here, I'll never be ready
to move toward the Light, the ultimate goal;
the Light that will feed and nourish my soul.

I want what I want, what will give the most pleasure;
I want it all and I don't want to measure and weigh
out my options and choose what is best;
I want what I want and forget the rest!

But the bright orange glow that warms me now,
can be mine forever; I know it somehow.

Balance is needed so I can move up;
and I don't have to go with an empty cup.
For what is suppressed will always grow stronger
and to reach the Divine will take even longer.

I must find the center, the middle ground;
only then can I enter the Light when it's found.
The True Light above, still out of my reach;
so much to learn, and maybe to teach.

The Second Chakra Affirmation

I'm caught in a struggle between
self indulgence and
self denial.

I know what I should
and shouldn't be doing,
but I waiver between
'All' or 'Nothing'.

Neither one feels right.

I know what's good for me
and what's not
but it's so hard to change.

Please help me to
find the courage and strength
to take charge of
the urges that are clearly
not serving my best interests.

Show me how to enjoy
the pleasures of this life
without the need for
excess or deprivation.

Solar Plexus (Manipura) Chakra

Symbol: Ten petal Lotus flower

Location: Solar Plexus

Primary Drive: Power

Color: Yellow

Element: Fire

Sense: Sight

Associated Crystals: Amber, Citrine, Topaz

The Third Chakra

I strengthen.

Amber fire burning bright;
always ready for a fight.

Fire in my belly, power in my soul;
no one knows better than me,
and I am in control.

Master of my universe, Destiny is mine,
I decide the 'Yes' or 'No';
Control is so sublime.

But what about my principles?
Self direction plays a part.
Self absorbed and self serving
won't bring me to my Heart.

Willpower needs it's balance.

To serve or be a servant
are two very different things;
the first brings satisfaction,
the second just demeans.

I set my Will to my intent
to achieve the things I need.
My inner strength is the strongest force;
I use it wisely to succeed.

My true power is self mastery, the power over 'Me'.
The hardest fight I'll ever wage, but the sweetest Victory.

The Light is getting closer now,
it's starting to burn bright;
I'm getting nearer to the sun
and further from the night.

The Third Chakra Affirmation

I want to feel in control
but it seems I'm always
in conflict.

I feel guilty so
I say 'yes' when I want
to say 'no'. Then
I feel angry because I feel used.

Sometimes I feel powerful
and I crave the competition
because I know I can win!

But having to always win
is draining. Why does everything
feel like a challenge?

Please help me to recognize
when I need to stand up for
myself and when to let things go.

Help me to understand that
being a peaceful person
does not mean I'm weak.

Heart (Anahata) Chakra

Symbol: Twelve petal Lotus flower

Location: Center of chest

Primary Drive: Love

Color: Green (Pink)

Element: Air

Sense: Touch

Associated Crystals: Aventurine, Rose Quartz

The Fourth Chakra

I feel.

Like aventurine grass on a warm summer day,
or the breeze through the trees
that takes my breath away.

Love. So simple, so sweet;
my center, my connection to those that I meet
and share in this journey that we call Life;
Love lightens the load and limits the strife.

When I look at my loved ones
with eyes that shine,
my Heart's at it's best; so close to Divine.

It can lead me to happiness,
to kindness, to Love;
it can carry me up to the Light
that's above.

But it can lead me astray,
to pain and despair;
I must keep the balance, I must stay aware.

While Empathy and Sympathy
may sound the same;
only one can elevate,
the other restrain.

My Heart is the meeting place
of all that I am;
the center that directs me
to my Promised Land.

For without the blending of below and above;
I won't find the Light, the true path to Love.

The Fourth Chakra Affirmation

I want to love and be loved
but why does it sometimes hurt?

I give and give but never
seem to receive.
Am I not lovable?

I work hard to be accepted
and I do whatever I can to
make those that I love
feel good.

But it never seems to be reciprocated.

Please help me to discern
the difference between
'I love you' and 'I need you'.

Teach me to love unconditionally;
without judgment or preconceived
notions of how others
should act or react.

Show me the way to share a healthy
love that benefits me as well
as all the people in my life.

Throat (Vishuddha) Chakra

Symbol: Sixteen petal Lotus flower

Location: Base of throat

Primary Drive: Communication / Expression

Color: Sky Blue

Element: Ether

Sense: Hearing

Associated Crystals: Aquamarine, Celestine

The Fifth Chakra

I speak.

And my word creates
beauty or sadness, or joy that elates
or crushes and destroys that which it hates.

Truth or deception, or no voice at all;
words rushing out, or slowed to a crawl.

I question my past, ponder my plight;
have I been wrong or have I been right?

Then out of the blue I stand in my truth,
thoughts from today, or maybe my youth,
I put everything out there for all to see;
my voice has been found, I'm finally free!

Free to express the person I am,
not the one in the mirror,
that's only a sham. No, the person
I know better than anyone else;
the person I know as my True Self.

I can write, paint, dance or sing
my energy soars, my spirit takes wing!

But as always, balance is key;
Energy unchecked
can become Anxiety.

I go forward, move up
towards the clear celestine sky;
The Light's even closer...

I can see it with my Eye.

The Fifth Chakra Affirmation

Why is it so hard to express myself to others?

I know I have good ideas,
I know I have opinions.

But it seems that I struggle
to articulate what I think
and feel.

I fear rejection.

Maybe my thoughts aren't valid;
my ideas not good enough.

Sometimes I feel the need to
argue my point;
But this only seems to alienate me
from the viewpoints of others.

Please give me the confidence
to appreciate the things
I have to offer;
to recognize my gifts.

Help me know that what
I think, and feel, and say
has worth.

Give me the courage
to stand in my truth.

Third Eye (Ajna) Chakra

Symbol: Two petal Lotus flower

Location: Center of forehead

Primary Drive: Transcendence

Color: Indigo

Element: Inner sound

Sense: Extra Sensory Perception

Associated Crystals: Fluorite, Indigo Tourmaline

The Sixth Chakra

I see.

A glimpse of the Divine has now been mine
I see it in everything;
All is sublime!

The images!
Both grand and amazing.
All indigo blue;
some dazzling and dazing,
too good to be true!

Surely it's Heaven; am I finally here?
Suddenly everything's
seeming so clear!

Or am I escaping the
dull and the drear and
only imaging I'm really here?

Finding true balance surely will take
strong will and discipline
to try not to break.

Fear or Faith?
The test is now here.
Faith takes me up,
I cannot choose Fear.

Inspiration abounds,
I choose what feels right;
nature, meditation, I seek Love and Light.
I find out what fits with the authentic 'Me',
for my Eye is open;

I finally see.

The Sixth Chakra Affirmation

I sometimes feel disconnected from
the Divine
and I'm discouraged.

I have at times caught a glimpse,
but can't always distinguish if this
is true inspiration or
just my imagination.

Sometimes I feel overwhelmed
by everyday life;
the noise, the sights, the smells,
I just want to separate from it all.

Help me to see the Divine
in everything and everyone;
the Beauty and the Love in every situation.

Help me to recognize when I
am being pulled down
so I can refocus my Intent and move up
and closer to Source.

Give me the Faith and Trust
that I need to truly
see my Spiritual Path;
and the Courage to stay the course.

Crown (Sahasrara) Chakra

Symbol: Thousand petal Lotus flower

Location: Top of the head

Primary Drive: Surrender to the Divine

Color: Violet or White

Element: Inner light

Sense: Empathy

Associated crystal: Clear Quartz

The Seventh Chakra

I know.

I'm finally here and
I know what I need.
Divine Direction
Is what I shall heed.

I understand now what it is that I crave;
I must simply surrender,
no need to be brave for Faith in
my Source has taken me here.
I Trust and Believe; there is nothing to fear.

Violet and white light
I float like a feather, but now,
to reality I must tie a tether!

To loose balance here is a dangerous thing;
Nirvana or madness,
which will it bring?

My roots must stay grounded
as I soar to this height;
The earth is beneath me,
I cannot loose sight.

Spring water, silver rain,
quartz crystal so clear;
to the Divine
I have now drawn so near.

I will not go back, I will not retreat;
for within Myself

I now am Complete.

The Seventh Chakra Affirmation

What's blocking me?

I want so badly to connect
with Source; I'm so close, but
something keeps getting in the way.

I try and I try and at times
I succeed! And I feel
the Love and the Power and
everything is perfect and beautiful!

And then it fades.

And all that's left are
questions without answers
and a sense of loss.

Am I trying too hard to control my journey?
Am I getting in my own way?

Please help me to know
when ego is reaching up and
pulling me down.

Help me to recognize that I
am the obstacle that blocks
my path to Enlightenment,
and help me to step aside.

The Mandalas